Singing Rails

Railroadin' Songs, Jokes & Stories
by
Wayne Erbsen

Jim Bollman Collection

Order No. NGB-900   ISBN:1-883206-26-X

I

Contents

A traveler must have a falcon's eye, an ass's ears, an ape's face, a merchant's words, a camel's back, a hog's mouth and a stag's legs.

-English proverb, 16th century

Railroad Superstition

If you walk sixteen railroad ties without falling off the rail, any wish will come true.

RAILROAD FEVER

It seemed the whole nation was under the spell of "Railroad Fever." Spanning the continent with the first transcontinental railroad, trains literally changed the face of America and conquered the frontier. As the most important machine of the 19th century, there were few aspects of American life untouched by the railroad. Even our dreams were affected. Where boys once longed to become a soldier, a sailor, or a cowboy, suddenly, they dreamed of becoming an engineer.

The men who worked the railroads fancied themselves a breed apart. Manning powerful "Iron Horses," they were immersed in the greatest adventure of the age. Working their way up the ladder, many seasoned railroaders started as young boys. Teams of youngsters, known as "news butchers," peddled their wares up and down the aisles of passenger coaches. The engineer often started as a wiper, who swabbed caked oil from greasy locomotives. A conductor's career in railroading might begin as a brakeman whose job often meant teetering atop rolling freight cars. Others worked their way up from telegrapher, switchman, brakeman, baggageman, fireman, station agent and yardman to conductor.

Railroadin' was seriously dangerous work. Railroad men braved Indian attacks on the great plains, blizzards in Montana, tornadoes in Nebraska, switchbacks in the Cascades, snows in the Sierras, and deserts in Nevada and Utah. Other hazards included train robbers, prairie fires, runaway trains, damaged bridges, and train wrecks. No wonder in a single month in 1888, 2070 railroaders lost their lives on the job, and another 20,148 were injured.

The songs, the stories, and even the jokes all play a part in telling the history of railroading. Although no one can say precisely when the first railroad stories and jokes were told, railroad music for the piano was published in Baltimore as early as 1828. Even the newfangled Edison cylinder "talking machines" of the 1890's celebrated the railroad with such popular songs as "A Night Trip to Buffalo."

Singing Rails is itself a train. Each page is a boxcar or passenger car loaded with the songs, the jokes and the stories of the people who lived the railroadin' life. Hop aboard, stranger. Let's go for a ride.

3

Cannonball Blues

It was in all the newspapers on the morning of September 7, 1901. The previous day, President William McKinley had been shot twice by anarchist Leon Czolgosz. Police were holding the assailant and had confiscated his weapon, a .32 Iver Johnson pistol. Within a week, the President had died and Vice President Theodore Roosevelt had taken over the nation's highest office.

These events set in motion the creation of a ballad about the assassination. Known as "White House Blues," it was eventually recorded on September 20, 1926 by Charlie Poole and the North Carolina Ramblers. The popularity of "White House Blues" spread and portions of the song showed up in the lyrics and melody of a seemingly unrelated song, "Cannonball Blues." It was the Carter Family, from Maces Springs, Virginia, who first recorded it in 1930 and again in 1935. The text and tune drew heavily on "White House Blues" and also contained fragments of older songs that had been collected as early as 1915. It is often performed as a finger-picking guitar showpiece.

Lis- ten to the train, com- ing down the line, Try- ing to make up all of her lost time From Buf- fa - lo to Wash- ing - ton.

You can wash my jumpers, starch my overalls,
Catch the train they call the Cannonball
From Buffalo to Washington.

My baby's left me, she even took my shoes,
Enough to give a man those doggone worried blues,
She's gone, she's solid gone.

Yonder comes the train, comin' down the track,
Carry me away but ain't gonna carry me back,
My honey babe, my blue-eyed babe.

I'm going up north, I'm going up north this fall,
If luck don't change, I won't be back at all,
My honey babe, I'm leaving you.

Lincoln's Ghost Train

Illinois legends tell that on the anniversary of the passing of Lincoln's funeral train, strange things happen. If you stand at the track where the train passes, the moon will turn dark. Far in the distance, you will then see the approaching lights and belching smoke of an oncoming train. As it passes, the locomotive will be draped entirely in black and the engineer appears to be a skeleton. The cars will all be darkened except the last, which is lit. Inside, you will see Lincoln's flag-draped casket with four Union soldiers standing at each corner, guarding it. When the train finally passes, the moon will become bright again.[15]

An old man with long gray whiskers came through the cars selling popcorn, chewing gum and candy. "Hey!" said one his customers. "I thought young boys were supposed to do your job." "I WAS A BOY WHEN THIS TRAIN STARTED."[6]

Michigan Central train caught in snowdrift, 1864

A Railroad Bible

Over 300 card sharks were reported working aboard the Union Pacific system alone. A deck of cards was so common it was often known as a "Railroad Bible." The Missouri Railroad threatened to fire any conductor who permitted gambling after one of its directors lost $1,200 to a card shark.

Casey Jones

It was early Monday morning, April 30, 1900. Engineer Casey Jones and fireman Sim Webb were determined to make up lost time when they left Memphis heading to Canton, Mississippi on the Cannonball. As the train highballed near Vaughn, Webb suddenly noticed the caboose of a freight train on the track ahead, and shouted a warning. As he hit the breaks, Casey's last words were, "Jump, Sim!" The fireman did jump clear of the train to safety, but Casey was still in the cab when his train plowed into the rear of the freight train, killing him and wrecking both trains.

The first song written about Casey Jones was apparently composed by Wallace Saunders, an illiterate black man who worked as a train wiper in the roundhouse of the Illinois Central at Canton. Before long, the ballad of "Casey Jones" was spread by railroad workers up and down the line. A version of the ballad even became a vaudeville hit in 1909, as sung by T. Lawrence Seibert and Eddie Newton, although neither Saunders nor Casey Jones' widow ever saw a red cent of the profits. Here is Seibert and Newton's version of "Casey Jones."

Come all you round-ers if you wa-nt to hear, A sto-ry 'bout a bra-ve en-gi-neer. Ca-sey J-ones was the ro-un-der's name, On a six eight wheel-er, boys, he won his fame.

Chorus

Ca-sey Jones, mount-ed to the ca-bin, Ca-sey Jones, or-ders in his hand, Ca-sey Jones, mount-ed to the ca-bin, And he took his fare-well tr-ip to the pro-mised land.

Casey Jones

"Put in your water and shovel in your coal,
Put your head out the window, watch them drivers roll,
I'll run her till she leaves the rail,
'Cause I'm eight hours late with that western mail."
He looked at his watch and his watch was slow,
He looked at the water and the water was low,
He turned to the fireman and then he said,
"We're goin' to reach Frisco but we'll all be dead."

   Casey Jones, we're going to reach Frisco,
   Casey Jones, but we'll all be dead,
   Casey Jones, we're going to reach Frisco,
   We're going to reach Frisco but we'll all be dead.

Casey pulled up that Reno Hill,
He tooted for the crossing with an awful shrill,
The switchman knew by the engine's moan
That the man at the throttle was Casey Jones.
He pulled up within two miles of the place
Number four stared him right in the face,
He turned to the fireman, said, "Boy you better jump
'Cause there's two locomotives that's a-goin' to bump."

Slang for Fireman

Ashcat, ash eater, bake head, banjo, bellringer, coal heaver, coaly, cut the buck, diamond pusher, dust raiser, goat feeder, grease ball, grease burner, handle the scoop, move dirt, rathole artist, scoop, smoke boy, soda jerker, stringer, stoker, tallow dip, tallow pot.

   Casey Jones, two locomotives,
   Casey Jones, that's a-goin' to bump,
   Casey Jones, two locomotives,
   "There's two locomotives that's a-goin' to bump."

Casey said just before he died,
"There's two more roads that I'd like to ride."
The fireman said, "what could they be?"
"The Southern Pacific and the Santa Fe."
Mrs. Casey sat on her bed a-sighin',
Just received a message that Casey was dyin'.
Said, "Go to bed, children, and hush your cryin',
'Cause you got another papa on the Salt Lake Line."

   Mrs. Casey Jones, got another papa,
   Mrs. Casey Jones, on that Salt Lake Line,
   Mrs. Casey Jones, got another papa,
   "And you've got another papa on the Salt Lake Line."

The Death of Edward Lewis

> "Only fools want to travel all the time.
> Sensible men want to arrive."   -Metternick

Though originally set to the Southern mountain tune "Sourwood Mountain," this version of "The Death of Edward Lewis" sports a spooky melody. The ballad was apparently written after Lewis' death in 1937 by Jack Hartley and sung around Asheville, North Carolina. Lewis was the engineer of the first engine on the Clinchfield R.R. #99. His train is said to have carried his coffin to his gravesite beyond Mt. Mitchell in the Nolichucky Valley of Tennessee. I learned the song from Dick Tarrier.

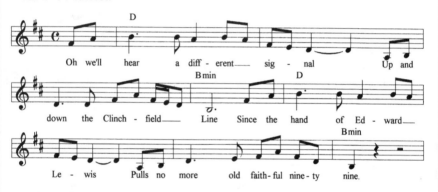

Oh we'll hear a diff-erent___ sig-nal Up and down the Clinch-field___ Line Since the hand of Ed-ward___ Le-wis Pulls no more old faith-ful nine-ty nine.

Now he's gone into the station
At the end of life's long run
Where there's joy and peace eternal,
For a life of labor that's well done.

But we'll miss him, yes, we'll miss him
Up and down the Clinchfield Line,
But we nevermore can call him back
To run old faithful 99.

It was up Nolichucky Valley,
Where the Linville River sweeps
Round the peaks of old Mount Mitchell;
She vainly calls for him that sleeps.

We will miss him and will wonder
If he sees the Clinchfield Line,
If he hears the plaintive calling
Of his dear old engine 99.

For he's gone into the station
Out beyond the twinkling stars,
Where there'll be no more worrying
Pulling trains of heavy loaded cars.

> *One stretch of track was so crooked we met ourselves coming back.*[6]

The Ant Who Stopped a Freight Train

Strange but true! In September, 1930, train number 41 of the Southern line was stopped by a red signal on the main line, though it had the right of way. It was finally discovered that a large red ant had crawled in between the contact points of the signal, and kept the train at a standstill. The ant, though fried, had stopped the freight train in its tracks.[13]

"The next train? It left ten minutes ago."

An engineer of a train loaded with cattle knew that the cowboy foreman had never been aboard a train before, so he decided to play a trick on him. He fired up the engine and whipped his train around the curves as if it were a blacksnake. The conductor of the train knew what was up and kept a close eye on the perspiring cowboy. When the ears of the foreman had taken on a slightly greenish color, the railroader inquired innocently if they were going too fast for him.

"Heck yes!" the cowboy exploded. "I don't know about the gent that's herding this thing, but personally, I'D RUTHER GET TO KANSAS CITY AN HOUR LATE THAN GET TO HADES ON TIME!"[3]

The East Bound Train

In an era of total and utter sentimentality, professional songwriters of the 1890's had a field day supplying the public with ballads which touched the heart and moistened the eye. In such a vein was "Going For a Pardon," with words by James Thornton and Clara Hauenshild and music by James Thornton. With the coming of the roaring twenties, however, the blush of popularity of the sentimental ballad began to fade. Flappers danced to the rhythms of a jazzy beat while the songs that had tugged at the heartstrings only a few years before now seemed relegated to a Tin Pan Alley waste basket.

At the same time that urban Americans were turning their backs on the old sentimental music, Southern rural singers embraced them. Growing up with parents who remembered and sang some of the maudlin English ballads, singers now embraced these sentimental songs as their own. They alone kept this type of mushy old-time song alive at the very time the rest of the country seemed bent on rushing headlong into the jazz age.

The first Southern musician to record "Going For a Pardon" was Dock Walsh of Wilkes County, North Carolina. In October of 1925 he recorded it for Columbia with lyrics that were considerably different from Thornton's original version.

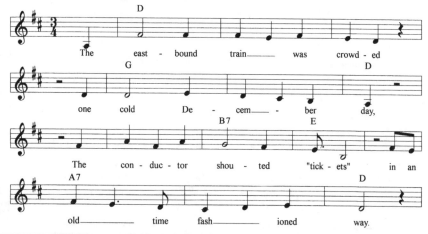

The East Bound Train

A little girl in sadness, her hair was bright as gold,
She says, "I have no ticket," just a little story told.

"My father, he's in prison, he's lost his sight, they say,
I'm going for his pardon, on a cold December day."

"My mother's daily sewing to try to earn our bread,
While poor dear old blind father's in prison, almost dead."

"My brother and my sister would both be very glad,
If I could only bring back my poor dear old blind dad."

The conductor could not answer, he could not make reply,
But taking his rough hand and wiping the tear drops from his eye.

He said, "God bless you, little one, just stay right where you are,
You'll never need a ticket while I am on this car."

The Legend of Daddy Joe

The greatest porter of them all was the legendary Daddy Joe. Of course, no one ever actually saw him in person, but stories of his adventures were told whenever porters gathered to swap tall tales. On one trip on the Central Pacific, hostile Indians attacked the train at a water tank. Daddy Joe is said to have climbed on top of his car and in thunderous tones talked the Indians into quiet submissiveness. Climbing down from the car, he then handed each chief and subchief a Pullman blanket. With the Indians subdued, the train went on its merry way.

Freight Train Boogie

*"If we stay at home and mind our business,
who will want railroads?"* -Henry David Thoreau

"Freight Train Boogie" is a "boogified" version of Casey Jones. It was composed by Rabin and Alton, the Delmore Brothers, under the pseudonyms of Jim Scott and Bob Nobar. Assisting them on their recording of the song was veteran performer Wayne Raney, who provided the train sound effects on his harmonica.

Ca-sey Jones was a migh-ty man But now he's rest-ing in the pro-mise land The on-ly kind of mu-sic he could un-der-stand Was an eight wheel dri-ver un-der his com-mand. He made the freight train boog-ie All the time He made the freight train boog-ie As he rolled___ down___ the line.

When the fireman started ringing the bell,
Everybody on the line could tell,
Casey Jones he was a-comin' to town
On a six-eight wheeler that was burning the ground.

He woke up the people all along the line,
Lord, how the man made the whistle whine,
He told his fireman, "You better hold your seat,
I'm gonna make this rattler do the boogie beat."

In 1925, when Happy Davis was set to begin working as a Pullman porter, he received this warning: "You won't see your family, hardly ever." His response was, "MORE POWER TO IT!" [17]

Buried Treasure!

It was the dark night of October 11, 1894. Just outside Sacramento, California, a hobo named James D. Harms was awakened from a sound sleep by the noise of digging and several men talking. Crawling out of his pup tent, Harms watched from a distance as two men hurriedly buried what seemed like large, heavy objects. When the men left, the hobo gleefully discovered the treasure the men had been burying: $51,000 in heavy gold bars.

What the hobo didn't know was that sometime before dawn, the two men had robbed the Overland Express. Their haul was too heavy to carry with them, so in their haste, they buried their treasure, vowing to return for it when the coast was clear.

The hobo managed to haul his treasure to a nearby town, where he proudly deposited it in the local bank. With his new found wealth, he outfitted himself in the finest duds. Among his new purchases were three mustache curlers! He soon traveled in style to New York, where he spent most of the money on women and wine. The rest he spent foolishly. Returning broke to San Francisco, he was finally tracked down by Wells Fargo agents and eventually received a sentence of three years in Folsom Prison.

The train robbers who got away, didn't. Turning to other robberies, one was killed by passengers during a botched robbery, and the second was killed by train detective Captain John Hume.[2]

Were They Lit?

The courtroom was packed with spectators as the jury was set to decide who was at fault in a railroad accident. The engineer whose train had rammed into the rear of another train swore he had not been flagged. The flagman on duty testified he had vigorously swung his lanterns to warn of the oncoming train. The sincerity and apparent honesty of the flagman swayed the jury in his favor.

Leaving the courthouse after the verdict, the flagman was congratulated for his steadfast testimony in the face of hostile questioning. "Well," began the flagman, "all I did was stick to the truth. I sure am glad he didn't ask me if the lamps were lit."[1]

While many train songs have the driving rhythm of a locomotive, "In the Pines," also known as "The Longest Train," is sung in a slow waltz time. Originating sometime around the Civil War, it was first recorded by Doc Walsh from Wilkes County, North Carolina in 1926. Later versions were recorded with such titles as "Black Girl," "The Longest Train I Ever Saw," "To the Pines," "Where Did You Stay Last Night?" "Look Up, Look Down That Lonesome Road," and "Don't Tell Me No Lie."

In the pines, in the pines where the sun nev-er shines,___ And I shiv-ered when the cold___ winds blow.

Little girl, little girl, don't lie to me,
Tell me, where'd you stay last night?

I asked my captain for the time of day,
He said he throwed his watch away.

It's a long steel rail and a short cross tie,
I'm on my way back home.

If I'd a-listened what mama said,
I'd never a-been here today.

A-lying around this old jail house,
Just sleeping my life away.

American Indians, alarmed over the railroad crossing their lands, often tried to stop passing trains. One Indian war party stretched rawhide lariats across the tracks between their ponies. They soon learned the raw power of a locomotive when the train kept right on going, dragging them and their ponies behind.

Railroad Superstition
Riding trains on Friday is bad luck.

Pioneer Logic

An engineer tried explaining to a pioneer the advantages the new line would bring him. To illustrate his point, he asked the pioneer, "How long does it take to carry your produce to market by muleback?" "Three days." "Then," said the engineer, "you can understand the benefit the railroad will bring to you. You will be able to take your produce to market and return home on the same day." "Very good," the slightly confused pioneer said. "But what shall I do with the other two days?"

Street-Car Salad

Never full! Pack 'em in!
Move up, fat man, squeeze in thin.
Trunks, valises, boxes, bundles,
Fill up gaps as on she tumbles.
Market baskets without number,
Owners easy-not in slumber.
Thirty seated, forty standing,
A dozen more on either landing.
Old man lifts the signal finger,
Car slacks up-but not a linger-
He's jerked aboard by sleeve or shoulder,
Shoved inside to sweat and moulder.
Toes are trod on, hats are smashed,
Dresses soiled, hoop-skirts crushed.
Thieves are busy, bent on plunder,
Still we rattle on, just like thunder.
Packed together, unwashed bodies,
Bathed in fumes of whiskey toddies;
Tobacco, garlic, cheese and beer
Perfume the heated atmosphere.
Old boots, pipes, leather and tan,
And if in luck, a "Soap-Fat man."
Aren't this jolly? What a blessing!
A Street-Car Salad, with such a dressing.
-HARPER'S WEEKLY, MARCH 23, 1867

Scribner's Monthly, 1888

Elephants to the Rescue!

In 1900 the South Park & Pacific Railroad was lumbering up the Colorado Rockies. In tow were cars from Barnum and Bailey's circus. Near the top of the mountain, the locomotive couldn't quite pull the load over the crest. To the rescue came two circus elephants who used their heads to push the train over the top.

Diamond Jim Brady left $2,500 in his will to his favorite porter.

John Henry

Considered America's best-known ballad, "John Henry" is said to be based on events that took place at the Big Bend Tunnel in Summers County, West Virginia, sometime between 1870-72. When a steam drill was brought in to replace a large number of workers, a contest was held. John Henry was chosen to go against the steam drill in the classic battle of man pitted against machine. In the end, John Henry drove fourteen feet while the steam drill only drove nine feet. Though victorious, his efforts cost him his life. As the song says, "He laid down his hammer and he died."

John Hen-ry was a lit-tle bit-ty boy Sit-tin' on his ma-ma's knee. Picked up a ham-mer and a lit-tle piece of steel, "Lord, ham-mer'll be the de-ath of me Lord Lord, A ham-mer-'ll be the death of me."

"The railroad will leave the land despoiled, ruined, a desert where only sable buzzards shall wing their loathsome way to feed upon the carrion accomplished by the iron monster of the locomotive engine. No, sir, let us hear no more of the railroad." —Tirade against railroad, ca. 1847.

John Henry

TRAVEL BY TRAIN

CHEAPER

THAN DRIVING
YOUR OWN
CAR

John Henry went upon the mountain,
Come down on the other side,
The mountain was so tall, John Henry was so small,
He lay down his hammer and he cried, "Oh, Lord"
He lay down his hammer and he cried.

John Henry was on the right hand,
But that steam drill was on the left,
"Before your steam drill beats me down,
I'll hammer my fool self to death
Lord, I'll hammer my fool self to death."

John Henry told his Captain,
"Captain you go to town,
Bring me back a twelve-pound hammer,
And I'll whup your steam drill down
I'll whup your steam drill down."

John Henry had a pretty little wife,
Her name was Polly Ann,
When John Henry got sick and had to go to bed,
Polly Ann drove that steel like a man,
Polly Ann drove that steel like a man.

They took John Henry to the graveyard,
And they buried him in the sand,
And every time that locomotive passed him by
Said, "There lies a steel driving man,
Lord, there lies a steel driving man."

Conductor Nicknames

Big O, big ox, boiler head, boiler wash, boss, brainless wonder, brains, brass buttons, cad, captain, conny, crumb boss, cushion rider, dinger, dud, gold buttons, grabber, hot-footer, ding, king pin, master, master mind, old man, shack's master, silk gloves, skipper, smart alec, swellhead, ticket snatcher.

Railroad Superstition
A sure cure for railroad sickness is a piece of stationery placed against one's chest.

Life's Railway to Heaven

"The swiftest traveler is he that goes afoot"
-Henry David Thoreau

The BUFFALO BILL

Convenient Service between

DENVER and YELLOWSTONE

AN OVERNIGHT TRAIN

Speedy tri-weekly service between Denver and Cody (eastern gateway to Yellowstone Park) during the Park season.

NORTHBOUND from Denver Mon. Wed. Fri. June 19 to Sept. 1	FAST 1939 SCHEDULE	SOUTHBOUND from Cody Tue. Thu. Sat. June 20 to Sept. 2
4:00 pm Lv.	Denver	Ar. 1:00 pm
4:59 pm Lv.	Boulder	Ar. 11:57 am
5:19 pm Lv.	Longmont	Ar. 11:33 am
5:50 pm Lv.	Loveland	Ar. 11:04 am
6:13 pm Lv.	Fort Collins	Ar. 10:45 am
7:35 pm Lv.	Cheyenne	Ar. 9:25 am
11:00 am Ar. Cody (Yellowstone) Lv.		7:45 pm

EXTRA VISITING HOURS

The above schedule gives Yellowstone Park passengers enroute to or from the East, several delightful hours sightseeing in and around Denver.

"Life's Railway to Heaven" started its long journey as a poem published in 1886 entitled "The Faithful Engineer," by William S. Hays. A professional songsmith, Hays is credited with such well-known compositions as "The Little Log Cabin in the Lane," "The Drummer Boy of Shiloh" and "Mollie Darling." His poem began, "Life is like a crooked railroad, and the engineer is brave..." It soon entered the folk process, with new verses being added to it. Before long it was forgotten that Hays had started the wheels rolling with his original poem.

In 1890 a song was copyrighted as "Life's Railway to Heaven," with words credited to M.E. Abbey and music to Charles D. Tillman. Though most of the lyrics are different from Hays' original poem, there is enough similarity to be sure that "Life's Railway to Heaven" began as Hays' poem, "The Faithful Engineer." In 1895 Hays himself republished his original poem, but this time he titled it, "Old Hayseed's Railroad Idea of Life." Apparently he didn't object, or didn't know, that his poem had become both a classic hymn and an enduring railroad song. It is now often entitled "Life is like a Mountain Railroad."

A Railroad Hero

Daring deeds of engineers were legendary. J. Harvey Reed was at the throttle over a railroad bridge when he saw a nine year old girl playing on the tracks up ahead. The little girl managed to lay herself flat on the ties just outside the rails. It was only the steps of the last car that brushed her off the bridge into the creek. Reed saved her by jumping off the moving train into the water below.

Railroad Superstition

To ward off bad luck, switchmen often carried in their left breast pocket the fuzzy foot of a graveyard rabbit killed in the dark of the moon.

Life's Railway to Heaven

Life is like a moun-tain rail-road, with an en - gi - neer that's brave, We must make the run suc - cess - ful from the cra - dle to the grave; Watch the curves, the fills, the tun - nel, ne - ver fal - ter, ne - ver fail, Keep your hand up - on the throt-tle and your eye up - on the rail.

Chorus Bless - ed sav - ior, thou will guide us till we reach the bliss-ful shore, Where the an - gels wait to join us in thy praise for- ev- er more.

As you roll up the grades of trial, you will cross the bridge of strife,
See that Christ is your conductor on the lightning train of life;
Always mindful of obstruction, do your duty, never fail,
Keep your hand upon the throttle and your eye upon the rail.

As you roll across the trestle look for storm or wind and rain,
On a curve or fill or trestle they will always ditch your train;
Put your trust alone in Jesus, never falter, never fail,
Keep your hand upon the throttle and your eye upon the rail.

As you roll across the trestle, spanning Jordan's swelling tide,
You behold the union depot into which your train will glide;
There you'll meet the superintendent, God the Father, God the Son,
With a hearty joyous plaudit, weary pilgrim, welcome home.

The Santa Fe lured passengers with the promise of meeting "successful men of affairs, authors, musicians, journalists, 'globe trotters,' pretty and witty women and happy children..."

The Lightning Express

It was an era dripping with sentimentality. Tin Pan Alley songsmiths gloried in trying to outdo each other with tearful ballads of dying newsboys, barefooted orphans, lonely mothers, and separated sweethearts. Within two years of Gussie Davis' successful railroad melodrama, "In the Baggage Coach Ahead," the songwriting team of J. Fred Helf and E.P. Moran composed and published "Please Mr. Conductor," in December of 1898.

Soon known as "The Lightning Express," the song was first recorded and released on cylinder by Byron G. Harlan in 1899. By March 8, 1924 it was recorded on Columbia by blind singer/guitarist Riley Puckett and on April 26th by blind Ernest Thompson. Within a year, it was also "waxed" by a number of important pioneers of early country music, including Fiddlin' John Carson, Ernest Stoneman and Vernon Dalhart.

The Lightning Express

The Lightning Express from the depot so grand
Had just pulled out on its way.
All of the passengers who were on board
Seemed to be happy and gay,
Except a young lad in a seat by himself,
Reading a letter he had;
'Twas plain to be seen by the tears in his eyes
That the contents in it made him sad.

The stern old conductor who passed through the car,
Taking tickets from everyone there,
Finally reached the little boy's side
And gruffly demanded his fare;
"I have no ticket," the boy replied,
But I'll pay you back some day,"
"I'll have to put you off the next station," he said,
But stopped when he heard the boy say: (Chorus)

A Grizzly Tale

A railroad agent in Northern California had been "balled out" by his boss for doing things without orders from headquarters. One day the boss received the following startling telegram: "Grizzly bear on platform hugging conductor. Wire instructions." [4]

A little girl in a seat close by
Said, "To put that boy off, it's a shame,"
So taking his hat, a collection she made,
And soon paid his way on the train.
"I'm obliged to you, miss, your kindness to me."
"You're welcome, I'm sure, never fear."
Each time the conductor came through the car
These words seemed to ring in his ear: (Chorus)

The Best, Worst Tippers

The base pay for porters around the turn of the century was about twenty dollars a month. Though tips varied widely, most porters agreed that foreigners, especially the English, were the worst tippers, followed by New Englanders. Women tended to be unpredictable in their tipping, but show people were usually the most generous.

Lonesome Pine Special

I t was to be a scorcher. Early in the morning of July 31, 1927, the A.P. Carter family climbed into their Model A Ford in Maces Springs, Virginia for the twenty-five mile trip to Bristol, Tennessee. It turned out to be a harrowing trip, which took all day. Driving on curvy mountain dirt roads, the Ford had to cross several creeks, and A.P. was forced to patch three flat tires along the way as each succeeding patch melted in the heat. Riding in the car besides A.P. was Maybelle Carter, his wife Sara, and two of their children, eight year old Gladys and a fussy seven month old, Joe. Also jammed into the car was an autoharp and a guitar.

The Carter Family was making the journey in response to a newspaper ad announcing that Mr. Ralph Peer of Victor Records would be holding auditions in Bristol. Arriving late in the day, the Carters found the location where the auditions were to be held. Thinking their simple country dresses out of fashion in such a big city, Sara and Maybelle snuck in the back door, to avoid being seen. Ralph Peer had more than fashion on his mind that day, and signed the Carters to a recording contract. They later recorded "Lonesome Pine Special" in Memphis, Tennessee on November 24, 1930.

I was walk - ing out this morn - ing With ramb - ling on my mind I am going to catch that spec - ial That train called Lone - some Pine.

Chorus
Take me back to Tex - as, Back to my old home.

Lonesome Pine Special

You can hear the whistle blowing
As it's coming down the line
That's the train I catch this morning
To ease my troublin' mind.

Oh I'm weeping like a willow
And I'm mourning like a dove
There's a girl way out in Texas
That I know I really love.

Oh, I'm going back to Texas
Where the lonesome coyotes whine
Where the longhorn cattle are roaming
Round that cabin home of mine.

Oh give me back my rifle
And give me back my gun
Give me back my home in Texas
And my ramblin' days are done.

The Lost Spike

James J. Hill, the railroad builder, was known to be exceedingly thrifty. One day, he was outraged to discover a new rail spike lying on a roadbed. With fire in his eye and the spike in his hand, he went looking for the section foreman. The quick-thinking foreman spotted his boss with the spike and hurried to meet him. "Thank goodness you found that spike, Mr. Hill. I've had three men looking for it for nearly a week!" [1]

Library of Congress

Cold??

In the early days of railroading, many poor youngsters in Bordentown, New Jersey earned a livelihood by selling hot bricks wrapped in blankets to shivering passengers.

Gandy Dancers

Union Pacific track layers were known as "Gandy Dancers." One legend tells of a man named Gandy, the boss of one of fastest track laying gangs, who did a shuffle or dance while tamping ties. Another story claims the shovel they used was made by the Gandy Shovel Company, and that the men "danced" out on the end of their shovels to level the track.

A man tried to kiss his wife goodbye as his train left New York. The train went so fast that instead of kissing his wife, he kissed a woman in Albany, some 150 miles away.

Farmers were lured to the arid plains of eastern Montana with promises that "rain follows the railroad."

Strange Railroad Laws

In the early days of railroading a law was enacted which read, "It is against the law for a train to enter the city limits unless preceded by a man on horseback."

• To keep cattle from grazing along railroad tracks, Arkansas passed a law against letting Russian thistles or Johnson grass go to seed along the track.

• Rhode Island made it illegal to run a passenger coach between the locomotive and a carload of dirt.

• Idaho passed laws requiring railroad workers to be able to read and write and imposed fines for not phoning home when their train was running late.

• A conductor who doesn't immediately eject a gambler in Minnesota can be arrested.

• In Maryland, it is illegal to "Knock a train off the tracks."

• It is against Montana law to show the movie "The Great Train Robbery."

• Los Angeles prohibits "firing on jackrabbits from the rear platform of a train."

• Connecticut law makes it illegal to lend out your handcar.

• It is a crime to salt a railroad track in Alabama.

• Texas law states: "Blankets must be washed every ninety days."

• One Kansas statute read, "When two trains approach each other at a crossing, they should both come to a full stop, and neither shall start up until the other has gone."[13]

The First of Many
The first train robbery was in October of 1866 when the Reno brothers, (Frank, John, Simon, Clinton and William) held up an Ohio and Mississippi train near Seymour, Indiana. Their haul was the tidy sum of $10,000.

Midnight Special

**"The light at the end of the tunnel
is the headlight of an oncoming train."**

To passengers boarding the Golden Gate Limited in Houston, this train was just a means to get where they were going. But to inmates some thirty miles away at the state prison at Sugarlands, the train meant freedom. When its headlights shown through the cold barred windows of their cell, maybe for a split second they could forget they were trapped behind bars. For an instant they could imagine they were being transported west in high style toward San Antonio, El Paso and points beyond.

The song we now know as the "Midnight Special" was collected in 1923 and was composed of fragments of older prison songs. Its earliest recording was in 1926 by Dave Cutrell backed by McGinty's Oklahoma Cowboy Band. The man most responsible for its popularity was Huddie Ledbetter, better known as "Leadbelly," who recorded it for John and Alan Lomax in July, 1934.

Midnight Special

MISSOURI PACIFIC LINES

Yonder comes my woman, how do you know?
I can tell her by her apron and by the dress she wore.
Umbrella on her shoulder, piece of paper in her hand,
Goin' down to the captain, says, "I want my man."

When you go to Houston, you better act right,
You better not gamble, and you better not fight.
Or the sheriff will arrest you, and he'll carry you down,
You can bet your bottom dollar, you're jailhouse bound.

Dumb-Struck

A country fellow was going to town to see his first train, and he decided to walk on the railroad track. The train came up behind him, and he took off down the track as fast as he could, just staying ahead of the locomotive. He ran all the way to town, where the train slowed and stopped. The depot agent who had watched him approach asked, "Why didn't you just get off the tracks?" The fellow gasped, "I knowed if I got off in that plowed ground, he'd catch me for sure."[5]

Unload!

When an engine was in imminent danger of catastrophe, the engineer and his fireman often had no choice but to jump to save their lives. It was always the engineer's call when to "unload." After one such horrific jump to avert sure death at the throttle of a run-away engine, engineer Henry French limped back to the telegrapher's shack and borrowed the telegraph key to tap out his own resignation, effective immediately.

With a name like the New River, it is ironic that this river is the world's second oldest, after the Nile. Running northward, it cuts a wide swath through parts of North Carolina, Virginia and West Virginia. The song likely originated in the late 1880's in Southwest Virginia and was first recorded in December 1923 by Henry Whitter, a harmonica and guitar player from Fries, Virginia. For over a hundred years the song has enticed singers to make up new verses. My contribution is the last verse. You can add yours after that...

Chorus

I'm rid-ing on the New Riv - er train

I'm rid-ing on the New Riv - er train

It's the same old train that brought me

here And it's soon gon - na car-ry me a - way

While visiting New Zealand on a tour in the late 'nineties, Mark Twain found that the trains were exceedingly slow-moving. One day he caught a train that seemed unusually slow, even for New Zealand. When the conductor finally came around, Mark promptly handed him half a ticket which was customarily used for juvenile passengers. The official looked hard at the white-haired, bushy mustached humorist and demanded somewhat sarcastically, "And are you a child?" "No, not any more," replied Twain. BUT I WAS WHEN I GOT ON YOUR DERN TRAIN."

New River Train

Darling you can't love one (2X)
You can't love one and have any fun
Oh Darling you can't love one.

Darling, you can't love two (2X)
You can't love two and still be true
Darling you can't love two.

Darling, you can't love three (2X)
You can't love three and still love me
Darling you can't love three.

Darling you can't love four (2X)
You can't love four and love me anymore
Darling you can't love four.

Darling you can't love five (2X)
You can't love five and get honey from my beehive
Darling you can't love five.

Darling you can't love six (2X)
You can't love six, that kind of love don't mix
Darling you can't love six.

Darling you can't love many (2X)
You can't love many or you won't get any
Darling you can't love many.

There was a young fellow on the train who couldn't find a seat. He was walking up and down the aisle, all the while cussing a blue streak. A preacher who was sitting near the aisle spoke to the young man. "Do you know where you are going, sir? You are going straight to purgatory." The young man said, "I don't care. And besides that, I've got a round trip ticket."[6]

A Good Chew

"A fellow sitting in the seat next to me was spitting tobacco juice on the floor. Every time the conductor walked by, he would notice it. Finally he came up to me and said, "Is that you that has been spitting tobacco juice on the floor?" The fellow in the next seat spoke up and said, "I spit that tobacco juice on the floor." The conductor then said, "YOU ARE THE FELLOW I'VE BEEN LOOKING FOR ALL DAY; GIVE ME A CHEW."[9]

Railroad Superstition

If you see two chickens fighting as you are leaving on a journey, your trip will be a safe one.

Nine Hundred Miles

Jimmie Rodgers

The exact origins of "Nine Hundred Miles" remain a mystery. To stymie serious research, there are at least three songs whose verses are interchangeable: "Train 45," "Reuben's Train" and "Five Hundred Miles." As if that weren't enough, the old song, "Gospel Plow," uses a similar melody for its verses. To give "Nine Hundred Miles" a needed chorus, I have borrowed the melody of the chorus of "Gospel Plow" and added it to "Nine Hundred Miles."

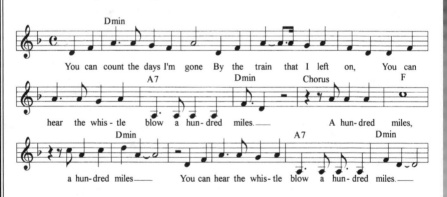

You can count the days I'm gone By the train that I left on, You can hear the whis-tle blow a hun-dred miles. A hun-dred miles, a hun-dred miles You can hear the whis-tle blow a hun-dred miles.

A Cash Crop

The Hole in the Wall Gang, led by Butch Cassidy and the Sundance Kid, had their own style of robbing trains. On June 2, 1899 they flagged down the Union Pacific with a red lantern, a signal of danger. Then they ordered the engineer to cut the express and baggage cars loose from the rest of the train and to pull them over a bridge several miles ahead. With dynamite, they blew up the bridge to foil pursuit by the rest of the train. When the agent resisted handing over the loot, they blew up the express car, scattering bank notes over the countryside. They harvested a "cash crop" of $60,000 and vamoosed.

Nine Hundred Miles

If my baby says so, I'll railroad no more,
I'll sidetrack my train and go home.

Lord, I'll pawn you my watch, and I'll pawn you my chain,
I'll pawn you my gold diamond ring.

You can count the days I'm gone by the train that I left on,
You can hear the whistle blow a hundred miles.

If that train runs right I'll be home tomorrow night,
Lord, I'm nine hundred miles from my home.

If the train runs right, I'll be home tomorrow night,
For I ain't gonna be treated this-a way.

Arrangement Copyright © 1997 by Wayne Erbsen. Fracas Music Co. (BMI)

Are We Having Fun Yet?

"I dislike the sleeping car sections more than I have ever disliked, ever shall dislike, or ever can dislike, anything in the world."   -Helen Hunt Jackson.

Somewhere west of Dodge City a discouraged prospector boarded a train. The conductor asked where he was going and the old-timer quickly answered, "Hell." Without hesitating, the conductor replied, "That will be sixty-five cents, and get off at Dodge City."

"**N**ine Pound Hammer" is like an empty freight car let loose at the top of a steep hill. As it careened down the mountain, gaining speed as it went, it picked up hitchhiking verses along the way. Some of these verses came from such songs as "Swannanoa Tunnel," "Take This Hammer," and "Roll on Buddy." The first commercial recording of "Nine Pound Hammer" was in 1927 by Al Hopkins and His Buckle Busters.

Chorus

This nine pound ham - mer Is a lit-tle too hea - vy For____ my size Bud - dy for my size.____

Take this hammer, give it to the captain,
Tell him I'm gone, tell him I'm gone.

If he asks you where I went to,
You don't know, buddy, you don't know.

There ain't no hammer in this mountain,
Rings like mine, buddy, rings like mine.

Rings like silver, it shines like gold,
It rings like silver, and it shines like gold.

Roll on buddy, try to make your time,
For I'm broke down, and I can't make mine.

Now, this old hammer, it killed my buddy,
But it can't kill me, buddy, it can't kill me.

"Run for the roundhouse, Nellie, he can't corner you there."

A Good Cigar

One time I was riding on a train, smoking a strong cigar. A lady sitting alongside of me said, "Will you please put out the cigar?" I put it out. I had on a new pair of shoes that were killing my feet. I pulled off one shoe and began rubbing my foot. It wasn't two minutes before the lady said, "Will you please light the cigar?"[6]

Beware of Card Sharks!

Some Pullman conductors passed out slips to passengers that read: "It is dangerous to play cards with strangers."[10]

> *The train ran so slow, one of the passengers got frustrated and tried to commit suicide. He ran ahead for a half mile and laid down on the track, but he starved to death before the train got there.*[6]

GENTLEMEN ARE REQUESTED
NOT TO SPIT ON THE STOVE (1859)

On The Dummy Line

CANADIAN NATIONAL RAILWAYS

Though a long list of definitions of the word "dummy" would include "blockhead" and "mannequin," the "dummy" in this song has more obscure origins. Some sources give its meaning as a train carrying railroad employees. Others say "dummy" was a term for open California streetcars. Several sources claim that the song referred to the Augusta Railroad of Augusta, Arkansas, which was built in 1918. It was first published in 1885 as "Riding on the Dummy," written by Sam Booth and Frederick G. Carnes.

This version of the lyrics is from the 1930 recording by the Pickard Family for the American Record Corporation. The melody was influenced by Uncle Dave Macon who in 1926 recorded a version based on one of his favorite subjects, Henry Ford's Model T.

Some folks say that the dum-my won't run, Now,
let me tell you what the dum-my done done.
Left Saint Lou-is 'bout half past one,
Rolled in-to Mem-phis at the set-tin' of the sun. On the
dum-my, on the dum-my line,
Ride and shine on the dum-my line,
Ride and shine and pay my fine When I
ride in-to Mem-phis on the dum-my line.

On The Dummy Line

Look Before You Leap

In the 1830's, trains stopped before nearly every curve. Engineers often sent a fire boy ahead to check the tracks for obstructions and on-coming trains.

Got on the dummy and I had no fare,
Conductor yelled, "What you doin' in here?"
I jumped up and I made for the door,
He smacked me on the head with a two-by-four.

Oh, the dummy rolled down that twenty-nine hill,
Blowed the whistle with a mighty shrill.
Stuck his head out the window, looked down the track,
You oughta seen the little dummy ball the jack.

Library of Congress

Drawn by Arthur Lumley, wood engraving by Knapp-Co., 1869

A passenger was sitting alongside a tired-looking fellow who was covered with feathers. "I say, good man, why are you covered with feathers?" "I was picking chickens yesterday and I was afraid to go to bed last night. I was afraid I would just lay there."[6]

Railroad Bill

Morris Slater, known as Railroad Bill, started robbing trains in rural Alabama and Florida in 1894. Armed with a rifle and two pistols, his modus operandi was simple. He'd board a train, locate items to steal, and then throw them out the open boxcar doors. At his leisure, he would go back along the track to gather in the spoils. To poor blacks in rural Alabama, he was a folk hero who left food on their doorsteps. Some claimed he was endowed with super-human powers and swore only a solid silver bullet could kill him. Others claimed he could change himself into different animals to elude capture.

With the law after him, Railroad Bill was finally tracked to Atmore, Alabama, where he was spotted at Ward's General Store eating cheese and crackers. Constable McGowan shot and missed Bill. While Bill was grabbing his own pistol, the storekeeper, Bob Johns, mortally wounded him.

Though Railroad Bill passed on to that hoosegow in the sky, the song about him still lives! The first recording of "Railroad Bill" was on September 11, 1924 by Riley Puckett and Gid Tanner.

Rail-road Bill, migh-ty bad man, Shot the lan - tern from the brake-man's hand, And it's ride,___ ride,___ ride.

> At the end of the nineteenth century, the Missouri legislature spoiled the fun of bored teenage pranksters by passing a law against soaping railroad tracks, which caused trains to slip back down a grade.

Railroad Bill

The Haunted Tracks

A train wreck in San Antonio claimed the lives of a number of passengers, including several children. They say the trees growing near the sight of the accident became stunted and twisted away from the tracks. For years, thrill-seeking local teenagers would put baby powder on the bumpers of their cars and slowly drive over the tracks where the accident occurred. Some claimed they could see tiny handprints in the powder. This became a nuisance when the area became littered with empty bottles of baby powder.[14]

Railroad Bill, sittin' on a hill,
He never worked and he never will,
And it's ride, ride, ride.

Early one morning, standing in the rain,
Around the curve come an old freight train,
And it's ride, ride, ride.

Railroad Bill, standing on a hill,
Lighting cigars with a ten-dollar bill,
And it's ride, ride, ride.

Railroad Bill, so mean, so bad,
Stole all the chickens that poor farmer had,
And it's ride, ride, ride.

Got a .38 special on a .44 frame,
How can I miss when I got dead aim,
And it's ride, ride, ride.

It was down in the state of Arkansas I rode on the slowest train I ever saw. It stopped at every house. When it come to a double house, it stopped twice. It made so many stops I said, "Conductor, what have we stopped for now?" He said, "There are some cattle on the track." We ran a little ways further and stopped again. I said, "What is the matter now?" He said, "We have caught up with those cattle again."[6]

The Railroad Corral

> "If an ass goes traveling, he'll not come home a horse."
> -Thomas Fuller (1732)

The long trail drives that began in Texas after the Civil War had their terminal point in cow towns like Abilene, Wichita and Dodge City. Such railheads provided the scenes captured in "The Railroad Corral." Written by Joseph Mills Hanson in 1904, it was quickly collected as being a traditional cowboy song by John Lomax, and included in his 1910 collection of cowboy ballads. The first two lines of the song show traces of "Rye Whiskey," a tune that was popular with the cowboys.

We're up in the morn - ing at break - ing of day. The chuck wa - gon's bu - sy, the flap - jacks in play. The herd is a - stir o - ver hill - side and vale, With the night rid - ers crowd - ing them on - to the trail.

Dirty Deck

A gunfight erupted during a poker game held in the caboose of a cowtrain when one cowboy said, "I don't like to play with a dirty deck." The dealer, who was none too clean himself, understood him to say "dirty neck." When the shooting was over and the smoke had cleared, one dead cowboy learned the importance of enunciation."

The Railroad Corral

Come take up your cinches and shake out your reins,
Come wake your old bronco and break for the plains.
Come roust out your steers from the long chaparral,
For the outfit is off to the railroad corral.

Slang for Caboose

Animal car, ape wagon, bazoo wagon, brain cage, chariot, chuck wagon, clown wagon, cook shack, coop, cracker box, crib, crow's nest, crumb box, crummy, doghouse, doodle bug, flophouse, glory wagon, go-cart, hack, hay wagon, hearse, hut, louse cage, monkey cage, palace, parlor, penthouse, possum belly, sun parlor, zoo.[16]

The afternoon shadows are starting to lean,
When the chuck wagon sticks in a marshy ravine.
The herd scatters farther than vision can look.
You can bet all the punchers will help out the cook.

But the longest of days must reach evening at last,
The hills are all climbed, the creeks are all passed.
The tired herd droops in the yellowing light;
Let 'em loaf if they will, for the railroad corral.

So flap up your holster and snap up your belt,
And strap up your saddle whose lap you have felt.
Goodbye to the steers from the long chaparral,
There's a town that's a trump by the railroad corral.

"A man who has never gone to school may steal from a freight car; but if he has a university education, he may steal the whole railroad."
                                                                                    -Theodore Roosevelt

Railroadin' & Gamblin'

"It is bad luck to pick up chips on Sunday."

When the names of all the greatest old-time country music performers are stirred around in a large tub, one name will always float to the top: Uncle Dave Macon. Known as "The Dixie Dew Drop," Uncle Dave began his recording career on Vocalion in 1924. Two years later, at the spry age of fifty six, he joined the Grand Ole Opry and became one of its biggest stars. A born performer with boundless energy, Uncle Dave delighted Opry audiences and radio listeners with expert banjo picking, jubilant songs, and down home humor.

Uncle Dave's version of "Railroadin' & Gamblin'" is a classic, although many of his lyrics are near-impossible to decipher. Scholars can only guess at some of the words he uses.

What your mam-my done told you Six months a - go

Keep on your coat and hat Be read - y to go. Oh,

rail - road - ing and gamb - ling Pick-in' up chip for mam - my,

Lord, Lord, Lord Stick your feet out Sam,

Kick-in' in the mud Stick your feet out Sam, Kick-in' in the mud.

Been in the state house	Lord that preacher said,	Got on the roadside
Been in that hall	"Ain't that a sin	Got on the track
Been in that courthouse	Johnny get your wood cut	Spent all my money
Worst place of all.	Lord here comes the wind."	No way to get back.

Strange Justice

RAILROAD
ILLINOIS TERMINAL
COMPANY

One of the most unusual train robbery cases in frontier history went like this. While being chased by a posse, John J. Moore stole a locomotive but jumped from the cab as it roared into a small town. The run-away engine plowed up a long length of track before it ground to a halt. Railroad officials knew they could not claim anything from the penniless train robber. Instead, they charged him with theft of the engine. Moore's attorney shrewdly argued that under ancient English law, a man could enter another man's house, move his goods from one side to another, and be charged with damage, but not theft. Therefore, he triumphantly told the jury, as long as the locomotive had not been removed from the tracks, Moore had not stolen the engine. It took the jury two minutes to acquit the "desperate" train robber.[7]

Jim Bob Tinsley

There were three kinds of passengers who rode the train, First Class, Second Class, and Third Class. I said "Conductor, what is the difference between the First Class and Third Class passengers? Aren't they all riding in the same car?" He said, "Just wait a while and I will show you." We ran a little ways and stopped again. The conductor came in and said, "First Class passengers, keep your seats; Second Class passengers, get off and walk; Third Class passengers, get off and push."[6]

Unlike many of the songs of the Carter Family which drew from 19th century sources, "Railroading on the Great Divide" was composed by Sara Carter Bayes. Recorded for Acme at radio station WOPI in Bristol, Tennessee on March 7, 1952, the session included Sara and A.P. Carter along with their children, Janette and Joe Carter. It is one of a small number of railroad songs sung in waltz time.

Chorus

Rail road ing on the great di - vide
Noth - ing a - round me but Rock - ies and skies,
There you'll find me as the years go by, Rail -
road - ing on the great di - vide.

Nineteen and sixteen I started to roam
Out in the West, no money, no home,
I went drifting along with the tide
I landed on the great divide.

Ask any old timer from old Cheyenne,
Railroad in Wyoming's the best in the land,
The long steel rails and short cross ties
I laid across the great divide.

As I looked out across the breeze
Number three's coming, the fastest on wheels
Through old Laramie she glides with pride
And rolls across the great divide.

A lady handed the conductor two tickets, one whole ticket and a half ticket. He said, "Who is the half ticket for?" She said, "My boy." The conductor said, "He's not a boy; he's a man. Under twelve, half fair, over twelve, full fair." She said, "HE WAS UNDER TWELVE WHEN WE STARTED."[6]

Joe Baldwin's Light

The date was 1867. The place was Maco, North Carolina. Flagman Joe Baldwin was riding alone that night in the caboose of a freight train when he heard a sound and noticed his car had become uncoupled from the rest of the train. As his car glided helplessly down the track, Joe looked up and saw a sight that sent shivers up and down his spine. Coming up fast behind him was the headlight glare of a fast passenger train, quickly bearing down on Joe's car. Grabbing his lantern, Joe began frantically swinging his lantern, trying to warn the engineer that a collision was imminent. Too late. As the caboose crossed a trestle over a swamp, the passenger train plowed into Joe's car, decapitating him. They say Joe's head was never found, and they buried his body without it. Soon after the accident, a light resembling a lantern started appearing near the swamp. Some say it was Joe, returning with his lantern, searching for his head. Among those who saw the strange light was President Grover Cleveland, who passed through Maco in 1889. A local psychic even claimed to have conversed with Joe in her living room.

New York Public Library

A Most Unusual Scheme

A gambler named Canada Bill Jones once offered the Union Pacific $10,000 for an exclusive one-year concession to three-card monte aboard their trains. To sweeten the deal, Jones promised to prey only on traveling salesmen and Methodist preachers. To their credit, the U.P. turned him down.

Reuben's Train

When old-time musicians gather to swap tunes and tales, some fiddler or banjo player will eventually drag out a version of "Reuben's Train." Popular since 1898, it uses such aliases as "Train 45," "Nine Hundred Miles," "Old Reuben" and "Five Hundred Miles." Though the verses often drift from one version to another, the chief difference is that "Nine Hundred Miles" is usually played in a minor key, while the others generally stay in a major key.

Oh—— Reu - ben had a train, run from En - g - land to Spain, But he could - n't get a let - ter from his home.

If you don't believe I'm gone, watch this the train that I ride on,
Lord, I'm nine hundred miles away from home.

You oughta been up town when old Reuben's train come down,
You could hear the whistle blow a hundred miles.

I'm walking these ties, I got tears in my eyes,
And I'm tryin' to read a letter from my home.

If this train runs right, I'll be home tomorrow night,
Lord, I'm nine hundred miles from my home.

If I die a railroad man you can bury me 'neath the sand,
So I can hear the whistle blow a hundred miles.

You caused me to weep, you caused me to moan,
Caused me to leave my good old home.

Calvin Coolidge could be relied upon to give porters the same tip every time: 15 cents!

Texas Longhorns

D uring the Civil War, Texas ranches were left largely unattended. Every able-bodied man was either riding with Confederate General John Hood, or patrolling the Comanche frontier with the Texas Rangers. The breed of cattle left to roam wild for five years was known as the Texas Longhorn. With horns spanning eight to ten feet, they were quick as a jackrabbit, meaner than a snake in a skillet and as uncontrollable as a runaway locomotive. When no grass was available, they ate prickly pear and mesquite brush. When water was scarce, they plodded to the Gulf of Mexico or did without. During these lean years, their numbers actually increased under conditions that would have wiped out a less tough breed of cattle.

By War's end, Longhorn cattle were the only thing in Texas that was worth a hoot. When word got out that they could be trail-herded to Abilene and then transported by rail to rich eastern markets, the profession of cowboyin' began. Railheads were soon the site of feverish activity. By 1871 the Kansas Pacific Railroad was shipping out 600,000 steers a year from Abilene and Hays.

Railroad Signals

One short whistle: Stop
Two short whistles: Go ahead
Three short whistles: Back up
2 long, 1 short, 1 long whistle: Grade crossing
4 long whistles: Approaching junction
2 short, 1 long whistles: Meeting another train
A lamp moved up and down: All right, move on
A lamp moved round & round: Back the train
A lamp moved right and left across the track: Danger - Stop

Railroad Superstition

Counting the number of cars in a long freight train
will tell you the number of years you will live.

Rock Island Line

"BEWARE of Three-Card and Confidence Men!"

When folksong collector John Lomax lugged his portable recording equipment into southern prisons, he was walking new ground. No one had ever mined this a rich (and captive) resource. Among the wealth of blues, ballads, and worksongs Lomax collected from inmates was "The Rock Island Line." He collected it first in 1934 from black prisoners in Little Rock, Arkansas.

It was Huddie Ledbetter, better known as "Leadbelly," who popularized "The Rock Island Line" with his booming voice and twelve-string guitar. First discovered by John Lomax while serving time for murder, Leadbelly eventually won his freedom in part by composing and singing a song for the governor. His first commercial record was made in January, 1935 for the American Record Corp.

Oh the Rock Is-land Line___ is a might-y good road,___ The Rock Is-land Line is___ a road to ride,___ Oh the Rock Is-land line___ is a might-y good road, If you want to ride you got to ride it like you're fly-in', Buy your tick-et at the stat-ion for the Rock Is-land Line___ I may be right and I may be wrong, I know you're gon-na___ miss me when I'm gone.

I may be right and I may be wrong,
I know you're gonna miss me when I'm gone.

Well, the train got to Memphis just on time,
Well, it made it back to Little Rock at eight-forty-nine.

A-B-C double X-Y-Z,
Cats's in the cupboard but he can't see me.

DINING CAR
IN
OPPOSITE
DIRECTION

The James Boys' First Train Robbery

The notorious outlaws Frank and Jesse James first tried their hand at train robbery on July 21, 1873. They had received word that the Rock Island and Pacific Railroad, (known in song as "The Rock Island Line") was loaded with a $75,000 gold shipment. Seven outlaws lay in wait on a curve six miles west of Adair, Iowa. Loosening a rail, they tied one end to a long rope. When the train came along that evening, the outlaws yanked the rope, which dislodged the rail. Seeing the danger ahead, engineer John Rafferty went into reverse, but the engine turned over on its side, crushing Rafferty and injuring the fireman and passengers. The outlaws promptly lined up the dazed passengers and robbed them of their valuables. To their surprise, the outlaws discovered that the gold shipment was not on the train. Their take was a measly $3,000. The real haul would speed by on the repaired tracks some twelve hours later. This time around, crime didn't pay.

The conductor was the captain of the train. A jack-of-all-trades, on a single run he might attend to a sick passenger or an injured crew member, eject a card shark or deliver a baby. One conductor admitted using the same pocket knife to cut the umbilical chord of a newborn baby that he had just used to carve a plug of chewing tobacco.

Railroad Superstition
Never sweep out a caboose after dark.

Rags, Dog Hero

Rags was a one-eyed fox terrier mascot in the Chicago rail yards in the 1930's. One night while riding in the cab of a switcher, Rags suddenly jumped through an open window, seven feet to the ground, and ran excitedly ahead of the slow moving train. The engineer stopped the switcher and a crewman went down to investigate. There he found Rags barking at an unconscious man, stretched out across the tracks, near where the train had stopped. Rags had saved the drunk's life.[13]

PASSENGERS NOT ALLOWED TO STAND ON THE PLATFORM

A Railroad Romance

It was at a whistle stop known as Wood River, Nebraska in the 1870's. The entire population consisted of a settler named Bankers, his wife and infant daughter, a young school teacher named Emma, and the station agent.

Word came that a Sioux war party was in the area, so the agent tapped out an urgent message to Ogallala, some 165 miles to the west. The Indians' began their attack by setting fire to the Bankers' cabin, but he escaped with the school teacher to the refuge of an unused cattle car. The agent, meanwhile, barricaded himself behind the iron safe in the operator's shack. As luck would have it, the baby was sick with the colic and the adults were afraid the baby's cries would alert the Indians to their hiding place. Mrs. Bankers "soothed" the crying baby with twenty drops of opium-laced paregoric. Nonetheless, one Indian did enter the car and was killed with the butt end of Bankers' rifle.

The agent, meanwhile, was engaged in fierce fighting with the Indians, and suffered a severe leg wound by a Sioux bullet. As things were looking grim, a relief train, running without lights, arrived with a party of soldiers and Pawnee scouts and routed the Sioux. The ending? The schoolteacher later married the conductor.

> *"I do verily believe that carriages propelled by steam will come into general use, and travel at the rate of 300 miles a day."*   —Oliver Evans, 1813

Mark Twain & the Tramp

Out walking in Hartford one day, Mark Twain was approached by a tramp. "Could you give a fellow the price of something to eat, sir?"

"You unfortunate man," sympathized Twain. "Come on, I'll buy you a drink."

"I don't drink, sir."

"How about a cigar?"

"Look sir, I'm hungry and besides, I never in my life smoked."

"How would you like me to place a couple of dollars for you tomorrow on a sure-winning horse?"

"Maybe I've done lots of things wrong, but I never gamble," replied the derelict rather proudly. "Say, sir, how about a nickel for a cup of coffee?"

"Tell you what," answered Twain with sudden inspiration. "I'll stake you to a whole dinner if you let me introduce you to my wife.

I want to show her what becomes of a fellow who doesn't smoke, drink or gamble."

The Pacific Railroad, west of Omaha

In 1850 one legislature ruled that trains could run on Sunday only if the conductors passed through the cars reading the Scriptures to the passengers.

Swannanoa Tunnel

Shielded from the rest of the state by towering mountains, residents in Western North Carolina longed to connect to the rail system then being rebuilt after its near-destruction during the Civil War. The chief obstacle to the construction was Old Fort Mountain, just east of Asheville, North Carolina. The engineer chosen for the task of building the road to Asheville was ex-Confederate major James Wilson.

Construction of the road began in 1877. Armed with $880,000 in state funds and 500 black convict laborers, Wilson was undaunted by the fact that his roadbed would have to climb some 891 feet in elevation, winding through seven tunnels. As if that wasn't enough, the massive tunnel would have to be constructed through solid granite with a length of 1832 feet. To speed construction of this tunnel, Wilson attempted to bore toward the center of the tunnel from each end at once. His efforts were successful some two years later, when crews building toward each other connected the tunnels perfectly.

The construction of the Swannanoa Tunnel was not without its human costs. Estimates of fatalities of the convict laborers ranged from a low of 120 to a high of 400. The song, "The Swannanoa Tunnel" was apparently composed and sung by crews building the railroad. The cave-in mentioned in the song perhaps refers to the accident of March 11, 1879 when Governor Zebulon Vance was notified that "daylight entered Buncombe County today through the Swannanoa Tunnel." Twenty three workers were killed.

The verses of "The Swannanoa Tunnel," were collected by Bascom Lamar Lunsford. The melody is compliments of Bucky Hanks, who learned it from his grandfather, who worked on the Swannanoa Tunnel.

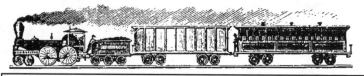

Railroad Insult
That locomotive couldn't pull a settin' hen off her nest.

Swannanoa Tunnel

Ashe-ville Junc-tion, Swan-na-no-a tun-nel All caved in, ba-by, all caved in.

I'm goin back to that Swannanoa tunnel
That's my home, baby, that's my home.

When you hear that watch dog howling
Somebody around, baby somebody around.

When you hear that hoot owl squallin'
Somebody dying, baby, somebody dying.

Last December, I remember
The wind blow cold, baby, the wind blow cold.

The hammer falling from my shoulder
All day long, baby, all day long.

Ain't no hammer in this mountain
Outrings mine, baby, outrings mine.

This old hammer rings like silver
It shines like gold, baby, it shines like gold.

Take this hammer and throw it in the river
It rings right on, it shines right on.

I'm goin back to the Swannanoa tunnel
That's my home, baby, that's my home.

OUCH!

Cowboys had the quaint practice of occasionally shooting out train headlights, caboose running lights and even brakemen's lanterns after sundown. Seasoned trainmen doused out their lanterns when approaching a particularly unruly cowboy camp.

Almond French was green at his job as brakeman, and learned about this precaution the hard way. One night his red lantern was shot right out of his hand. He was particularly irked that the shot that hit the lantern had first traveled between his legs!

La La Land

You didn't stop a moving train in a hurry. In fact, it took as much as 3,000 feet for a fifty car train traveling at forty miles per hour to stop. One engineer just managed to stop his speeding train in time to save a drunk who was passed out on the track. When they extracted him out from under the cowcatcher, he was still in la la land.

This Train

The idea of taking a train to Heaven probably originated soon after a preacher's sermon was interrupted by the sound of a noisy train going by. Some citizens even tried to ban train travel on Sundays entirely. Failing that, sermons and songs began cropping up which hailed the railroad as a sure way to get to Heaven or Hell ("The Hellbound Train").

"This Train" was first recorded as "This Train is Bound For Glory" in August, 1925 by Wood's Blind Jubilee Singers for the Starr Piano Company.

Chorus F

This train is bound for glo-ry, this train, This train is bound for glo-ry,

C7   F

this train, This train is bound for glo-ry,

Bb   F   C7   F

Don't car-ry nothing but the righteous and the ho-ly, This train is bound for glo-ry, this train.

Bill Evans, a well-known gunman, boarded a train at Dodge City. When conductor John B. Bender asked for a ticket, Evans pulled the larger of his two shooting irons and said, "This is my ticket, pass on." Bender passed on to the back of the car but only to pick up his sawed-off shotgun. Walking up the aisle behind Evans, he rammed it in the outlaw's back, saying, "I'LL PUNCH THAT TICKET NOW."[19]

This Train

*The train ran so fast, it took two men to see it - one to say,
"Yonder she comes," and the other to say, "There she goes."*[21]

Peace at Last!

*Two women on a
train argued about
the window and at
last called the porter
as referee. "If this
window is open," one
declared, "I shall catch
cold and will die."
"If the window is
shut," the other
announced, "I shall
certainly suffocate."
The two glared at
each other. The
porter was at a loss,
but he welcomed the
advice of a drunk
who sat nearby. Said
he, "First open the
window. That will
kill one. Next, shut it.
That will kill the
other. Then we can
have some peace!"*

This train don't carry no gamblers, this train (2X)
This train don't carry no gamblers,
No liars, thieves, no midnight ramblers,
This train don't carry no gamblers, this train.

This train don't carry no jokers, this train (2X)
This train don't carry no jokers,
No snuff dippers, no cigar smokers,
This train don't carry no jokers, this train.

This train don't carry no clinkers, this train (2X)
This train don't carry no clinkers,
No evil thinkers or moonshine drinkers,
This train don't carry no clinkers, this train.

This train don't carry old Satan, this train (2X)
This train don't carry old Satan,
Come on children, don't keep it a-waitin'
This train don't carry old Satan, this train.

*One "Whistle Stop" town had a steady population growth due to the whistle. It
blew every morning too early to get up, but too late to go back to sleep.*[19]

The Higher is Lower

A Texas cowboy boarded a train at Denver after having worked a trail drive. He walked in the sleeper with a bundle of blankets and asked the Pullman conductor if there was any place where he could bed down. The conductor told him he could have either the upper or the lower. The cowboy said any place would do for him, not knowing what was meant by the "upper" or "lower." The conductor droned on, saying: "The lower is higher than the upper. The higher price is for the lower, if you want the lower, you will have to go higher. We sell the upper lower than the lower. In other words, the higher the lower. Most people don't like the upper, although it is lower on account of its being higher. When you occupy an upper you have to go up to go to bed, and get down when you get up. You can have the lower if you pay higher. The upper is lower than the lower because it's higher. If you are willing to go higher, it will be lower." When the conductor finally looked around, the tired cowboy had already spread his blankets down in the aisle of the Pullman, using his boots and pistol for a pillow.

Harper's Weekly, 1880

Railroad Insult

He was so ugly he could make a train take a dirt road.[18]

The First Big Train Heist

The first big train holdup was led by the infamous outlaw Sam Bass. Well-liked for his generosity, Sam was a robber, gambler, race horse entrepreneur and whiskey guzzler. On September 18, 1877 a Union Pacific train stopped at Big Springs, Nebraska for water. With guns drawn, the outlaws made their move. The Wells Fargo agent bravely concocted a story that there was a time-lock on the safe, which would open only in Omaha. In frustration, Sam attacked the safe with an ax, but produced only sparks. One of the gang then discovered three wooden boxes stacked nearby. To their jubilation, they discovered the boxes were loaded with $60,000 in twenty dollar gold pieces. A smaller safe netted another $458. The passengers were shaken down for an additional $1,300. Never before had a train robbery produced such loot.

Harper's Weekly, November 1, 1884

Poker Alice

Among the more colorful card sharks to prey on railroad passengers was the fair-haired lass known as Poker Alice Ivers. Though her usual haunts were the gambling tables in western mining camps, she also plied her talents on unwary railroad passengers. They never suspected that behind her dainty frame was one of the most notorious gamblers of the Old West. Upon retiring to Deadwood, South Dakota, she set up a most unusual bordello. Every Sunday she closed her gambling hall and gave Sunday-school lessons to her employees.

Train on the Island

Though the circumstances surrounding "Train on the Island" remain a mystery, this song was popular before the turn of the century around Galax Virginia, and Mount Airy, North Carolina. A standard in most local fiddlers' tune bag, it was first recorded in 1927 by J.P. Nester and Norman Edmonds. I added the last three verses.

Train on the is-land, Thought I he-ard it squeal, Go and tell my true love,
I can't ho-ld the wheel, Go and tell my true love, I can't hold the wheel.

God's Highway

"Canals, sir, are God's own highway, operating on the soft bosom of the fluid that comes straight from Heaven. The railroad stems direct from Hell. It is the Devil's own invention, compounded of fire, smoke, soot and dirt, spreading its infernal poison throughout the fair countryside. It will set fire to houses along its slimy tracks. It will leave the land despoiled, ruined, a desert where only sable buzzards shall wing their loathsome way to feed upon the carrion accomplished by the iron monster of the locomotive engine. No, sir, let us hear no more of the railroad." [1]

Railroad Superstition
It is bad luck to begin a journey by train on Sunday.

Train on the Island

Train on the island
Thought I heard it blow,
Go and tell my true love
Sick and I can't go,
Go and tell my true love,
Sick and I can't go.

Train on the island
Thought I heard it squeal,
Go and tell my true love,
Happy I do feel, Lord
Go and tell my true love,
Happy I do feel.

Train on the island
Thought I heard it say,
Go and tell my true love,
I'm a-goin' away
Go and tell my true love,
I'm a-goin' away.

Train on the island,
Thought I heard it moan,
Go and tell my true love,
I am going home,
Go and tell my true love,
I am going home.

Train on the island,
Thought I heard it cry,
Go and tell my true love,
I am going to die,
Go and tell my true love,
I am going to die.

Afraid of fouling windows with soot from passing locomotives, many communities in the early days of railroading forbid trains from running through town. Special teams of horses stood ready to tow trains past the city limits.

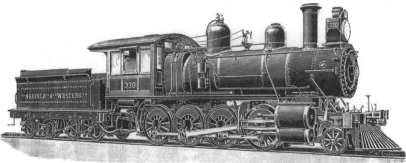

Norfolk & Western

The First Whistle

The origin of the steam whistle can be traced to the May 4, 1833 wreck that took place between Bagworth and Thorton, England. A market cart loaded with eighty dozen eggs and fifty pounds of butter was hit by The Samson, a pioneer locomotive. To prevent such accidents, railroad directors hired a musical instrument maker to build what was called a steam trumpet, which was later replaced by the steam whistle.

Train That Carried My Girl From Town

I t was the West Virginia guitar player, Frank Hutchison, who first recorded this song for OKeh records in September, 1926. This session utilized the primitive acoustic method of recording. In January 1927 he returned to the studio to record the song using the new electrical method.

Like many traditional songs, "The Train That Carried My Girl From Town" borrowed bits and pieces from earlier compositions. Some of these include, "Mean Conductor Blues," "Dink's Blues," "Hesitating Blues" and "I Wish the Train Would Wreck." Among those who went on to record Hutchison's version of the song were Doc Watson, Wade Mainer and Zeke Morris, Ola Bell Reed, Fields Ward and Ralph Blizzard. The version printed here is my own reworking of the chorus.

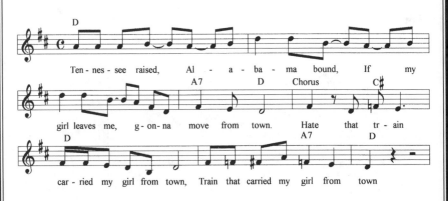

Ten - nes - see raised, Al - a - ba - ma bound, If my girl leaves me, g - on - na move from town. Hate that tr - ain car - ried my girl from town, Train that carried my girl from town

One time a distraught passenger asked the porter to come to his private berth. Every time the porter consoled him, the man gave him a tip. This went on for a while, and finally the man explained why he was so upset. "It's my daughter," he said, handing the porter another tip. "She has run away to New York to get married." "What's so terrible about that?" asked the bewildered porter. "Shouldn't you be happy?" "No" answered the man. "She married a Pullman porter." [17]

Train That Carried My Girl From Town

COLORADO AND SOUTHERN

Hate that train carried my girl from town,
If I knowed her number, sure I'd flag her down.
Where were you when the train left town?
Standin' on the corner, head a-hanging down.

Wish to the Lord that the train would wreck,
Kill the engineer, break the fireman's neck.
Hello, central, give me 6-0-9,
Want to talk to that gal of mine.

Breakfast on the table, coffee's getting cold,
Some old rounder stole my jelly roll.
Want no grease mixed in my rice,
That girl of mine took my appetite.

There goes my girl, somebody call her back,
She's got her hand in my money sack.
Ashes to ashes, dust to dust,
Show me that woman a man can trust.

Railroad Superstition

Eating a bean before going on a journey will bring you good luck.

A Gambling Man

George Devol was an infamous card shark who extracted upwards of two million dollars from unwilling passengers. His game was three card monte. Often caught using a marked deck, Devol had to defend himself with fisticuffs, firearms or occasionally leaping for his life from a speeding train in a hail of bullets. On one occasion, he killed a man by butting him in the stomach like a billy-goat. Devol once went head-to-head with a circus performer who specialized in butting down doors with his head. And he won!

Wabash Cannonball

Silverton Northern, 1899

Alan Lomax best described the mythical train known as the Wabash Cannonball: "Each tie was made from an entire redwood tree. The conductor punched each ticket by shooting holes through it with a .45 caliber automatic. The train went so fast that after it was brought to a dead stop, it was still making sixty-five miles an hour." The song was first printed in 1904 but it was based on a 1882 song by the name of "The Great Rock Island Route!" by J.A. Roff.

Reprinted from *Ozark Folksongs* by Vance Randolph, by permission of the University of Missouri Press. Copyright by the curators of the University of Missouri.

Chorus

G / C / D7

Lis-ten to the jin-gle, the rum-ble and the roar, As she glides a-long the wood-land, thru the

G / C

hills and by the shore. Hear the migh-ty rush of the en-gine, hear that lone-some ho-bo squall,

D7 / G

Trav-eling thru the jun - gle on the Wa-bash Can-non-ball.

Jack up the Whistle!

The Boggs River & Northern Railroad often asked miracles of O'Leary, its shop foreman. With old battered parts for supplies, he was expected to maintain and even revitalize broken down locomotives.

One day, old sorry looking No. 36 was brought in for O'Leary to bring it up to tip-top shape. He looked it over and fired off a dispatch with this advice: "Jack up her whistle and build a new engine underneath." [1]

Railroad Superstition

Never watch a train out of sight if it has a friend on it.

Wabash Cannonball

"Follow the Flag
WABASH

From the great Atlantic ocean to the wide Pacific shore.
From the queen of flowing mountains, to the south bells by the shore.
She's mighty tall and handsome and quite well known by all,
She's the combination of the Wabash Cannonball.

She come down from Birmingham one cold December day,
And she rolled into the station you could hear the people say,
There's a girl from Birmingham, she's long and she is tall,
She come down to Birmingham on the Wabash Cannonball.

Here's to Daddy Claxton, may his name forever stand,
And always be remembered in the courts of Alabam,
His earthly race is over and the curtains 'round him fall,
We'll carry him home to victory on the Wabash Cannonball.

> *Passenger: "Conductor, that fellow sitting opposite me is a lunatic. He claims he is George Washington."*
> *Conductor: "Be calm, lady; I'll take care of the matter. (Shouting) NEXT STATION, MOUNT VERNON."*

May 10, 1869 - Promontory, Utah

The American Railway, 1897

There's more than one way to get to Heaven. With the popularity of rail travel, many believed the night express would one day carry them to Heaven in grand style. A great spunky version of "When the Train Comes Along" was recorded in August, 1938 by the inimitable Uncle Dave Macon, early star of the Grand Ole Opry.

Some come walk-in' and some come lame, Gon-na meet you at the sta-tion when the train comes a - long; Some comes walk-in' in Je-sus' name, Gon-na meet you at the sta-tion when the train comes a - long.

Chorus Oh when the train comes a - long, Oh when the train comes a - long, I will meet you at the sta-tion When the train comes a - long.

Two hobos met. Said the first, "How are you, Mike?" "Terrible, just terrible," said the other. "Starvation is staring me right in the face." "Is that so," said the other. "It couldn't be very pleasant for either of you, I'm sure!"

When the Train Comes Along

Sins of years are washed away,
Gonna meet you at the station when the train comes along;
Darkest hour is changed to day,
Gonna meet you at the station when the train comes along.

Doubts and fears are borne along,
Gonna meet you at the station when the train comes along;
Sorrow changes into song,
Gonna meet you at the station when the train comes along.

Ease and wealth become as dross,
Gonna meet you at the station when the train comes along;
All my boast is in the cross,
Gonna meet you at the station when the train comes along.

Selfishness is lost in love,
Gonna meet you at the station when the train comes along;
All my treasures are above,
Gonna meet you at the station when the train comes along.

Railroad Ripoff

To gain additional revenues, railroads often charged outrageous rates, particularly when they had a monopoly. One farmer in Corinne, Utah ordered a plow from Chicago. Southern Pacific insisted on sending the plow past Corinne all the way to San Francisco and then back to Corinne. The farmer was obliged to pay freight both ways and missed the plowing season to boot!

Judge: "Have you been up before me before?"
Hobo: "I don't know, judge. What time do you get up?"

Ninety-Seven was an hour late when Engineer Joseph A. Broady and a fresh crew climbed aboard at Monroe, Virginia on September 27th, 1903. With two firemen to stoke the boiler, Broady was determined to make up the lost time. A more experienced engineer would have heeded the signs on both sides of the track approaching Stillhouse Trestle that read, "Slow Up, Trestle!" When the highballing mail train hit the curve before the trestle, it leaped the rails and plowed one hundred feet into the banks of a stream. Among the nine people killed were both firemen, the conductor, flagman, and several workers. As the song tells it, Engineer Broady was, "Found in the wreck with his hand on the throttle, scalded to death by the steam."

Considerable controversy surrounds the origins of the song, "The Wreck of the Old 97." Among the first to arrive at the scene of the accident was eighteen year old Fred Jackson Lewey. Not long after the accident, he claimed to have composed a song about it. Eventually, he sang it for Charles Noell, who set the poem to the 1865 song "The Ship That Never Returned," by Henry Clay Work. Noell then claimed the entire composition as his own.

"The Wreck of the Old 97" was first recorded by Henry Whitter in 1923 for the General Phonograph Corporation.

Well, they gave him his or-ders at Mon-roe, Vir-gin-ia, Say-ing, "Steve you are way be-hind time. This is not 'thir-ty-eight, But it's old 'nine-ty-se-ven, You must put her in to Spen-cer on time."

Wreck of the Old 97

PORT
ST JOE
ROUTE

He turned and said to his black greasy fireman,
"Just shovel on a little more coal,
And when we cross the White Oak Mountain
You can watch old 'ninety-seven roll."

An ignorant farmer boy on his first train trip was asked by the porter, "Sir, shall I brush you off?" "No, when the train stops, I'll just get off.[20]"

It's a mighty rough road from Lynchburg to Danville
On a line on a three mile grade,
It was on this grade that he lost his airbrakes,
You can see what a jump he made.

He was going down the grade makin' ninety miles an hour,
When his whistle broke into a scream,
They found him in the wreck with his hand on the throttle
He was scalded to death by the steam.

In 1931 a prairie cyclone picked up an entire train and carried it 100 feet from the tracks.

Now, ladies, you must take warning,
From this time now on learn,
Never speak harsh words to your true loving husband,
He may leave you and never return.

A Porter's Tip

A porter on a train was asked why rich men usually give smaller tips than poor men. "Well, sir," the porter answered, "the rich man doesn't want anybody to know he's rich, and the poor man doesn't want anybody to know he's poor."

The Talking Corpse

In 1886 a clever crook concocted what he thought was an ingenious plan to rob a train. Concealing himself in a coffin, he shipped himself aboard a Wisconsin express train, waiting for the opportune time for his robbery. A suspicious express agent, hearing noises inside the casket, piled heavy freight on top of the casket. At the next station the coffin was placed on the station platform. The express agent loudly addressed the casket; "Is there a man in that box? If so, he'd better speak. I'm going to shoot through it." The "corpse" quickly yelled, **"I'm in here, don't shoot!"** The sheepish looking robber was taken into custody and later received a three year prison sentence.[2]

Robbery on the Union Pacific

Right Hand Man

When a trainmaster hired a brakeman, he often asked to see his hands. If a finger or two was missing, the trainmaster knew the man was experienced.

The Curse of Alpine

CHICAGO & ILLINOIS MIDLAND

Angry over the destruction of their hunting grounds, the Ute Indians were said to have placed a curse on the Alpine tunnel which cut across the continental divide in Colorado. At 11,940 feet above sea level, it was the highest railroad pass on the continent. An 1884 snowslide, which engulfed a train and killed thirteen passengers and crew, was attributed to the Curse of Alpine. Due to heavy snows, the Alpine tunnel was closed from 1888 to 1895. When it finally reopened, the legend of the Curse of Alpine was rekindled when four members of the first train crew to enter the tunnel in seven years were killed by asphyxiation. The engineer, Dad Martinis, was found dead with his left hand on the air valve and his right hand on the reverse gear. Local residents say the tunnel is still haunted by his ghost.

Shoeless!

Late one night while running out of New York, porter Johnnie Jones broke company rules by gathering up all the shoes in his car and took them to the next Pullman to shine. After shining all the shoes to a high gloss, Jones attempted to return to his car but was shocked to discover that his car was gone! While he was shining the shoes, his car had been switched to another train. As far as we can tell, his passengers are *still* looking for their shoes.

Train wreck at Batavia, New York, 1885

Railroad Superstition

It is bad luck to count the cars when going around a curve.

Thanks!

One engine alone cannot pull a huge freight train. Invaluable help came from Norm Cohen and his ground-breaking work *Long Steel Rail, The Railroad in American Folksong.* Thanks also goes to Bob Willoughby for musical transcription, Steve Millard for design, Barbara Swell, Janet Swell and Lori Erbsen for editing. Thanks also to Tracy McMahon, Leanne Erbsen, Joe Bruno, David A. Brose, Terry L. Long, John Showalter, Jim Bollman, Susan Porter, Jim Griffith, Jerry Triplett, Joe Newberry and Ms. Fedock's 7th grade Literature class.

Sources

1. *The Story of American Railroads*, Stewart Holbrook, 1947; 2. *A Treasury of Railroad Folklore*, B.A. Botkin and Alvin F. Harlow, 1953; 3. Neil M. Clark, "God's Roundup," *Saturday Evening Post*, March 6, 1945; 4. *Desert Scrap Book*; 5. *More Laughter in Appalachia*, Loyal Jones, 1995; 6. *On A Slow Train Through Arkansas,* Thomas W. Jackson, 1903; 7. *The Authentic Wild West*, James D. Horan, 1977; 8. *The Trail Drivers of Texas*, 1925; 9. *Slow Train to Yesterday*, Archie Robertson, 1945; 10. *Railroads in America,* Oliver Jensen, 1975; 11. *Railroadman*, Chauncey Del French, 1938; 12. *The Twentieth Century Book of Toasts*, Paul E. Lowe, 1910; 13. *Off on a Wild Caboose Chase*, Adolf Hungry Wolf, 1988; 14. Collected by Susan Porter; 15. Collected by Robert Bailey; 16. *Language of the Railroader*, Ramon F. Adams, 1977; 17. *Miles of Smiles, Years of Struggle*, Jack Santino, 1989; 18. Dave Cohen; 19. *The Toastmaster's Handbook*, Herbert V. Prochnow; 20. *Corral Full of Stories*, Joe M. Evans; 21. *On a Fast Train*, Thomas W. Jackson, 1905.

Happy Rails!

> The time will come when people will travel in stages moved by steam engines, from one city to another, almost as fast as birds fly, fifteen or twenty miles an Hour."
> -Oliver Evans (1813)